I visit the bears.

I sit on their chairs.

Who am I?

I am Goldilocks.

Who am I?

Story by
Norah Clegg and Don Hughes

Pictures by John Lobban

Oliver & Boyd

I sit on a wall.

I have a great fall.

Who am I?

I am Humpty Dumpty.

I fell down
and broke my crown.
Who am I?

I am Jack.

I march them up
to the top of the hill.
Who am I?

I am the Grand Old Duke
of York.

I huff and I puff
and I blow the house down.
Who am I?

I am the big bad wolf.

Hey diddle diddle
the cat and the fiddle.
I jumped over the moon.
Who am I?

I am the cow.

Hickory dickory dock.
I ran up the clock.
Who am I?

I am the mouse.